The Financial Fortress Plan

Keeping Your Money Safe During A Dollar Reset & Devaluation

By Dennis Stapp

This educational report was written for **THE MADISON INSTITUTE ASSOCIATION (TMI)** as a public service, and all right are reserved. Referenced excerpts are permitted and limited to 100 words without written permission.

TMI is a non-profit organization. If you like this report we ask you to support us by buying the book Anger to Action **by The Madison Institute Association; which is available at Amazon.com in softback and** Kindle **formats.**

All websites referenced are accurate at the time of writing but may change in the future or cease to exist. The referencing of websites and resources does not in any way imply author or publisher endorsement of the site's contents, or website owner's endorsement of this book.

Groups and organizations mentioned are for informational purposes, and listing does not imply publisher or author endorsement of their activities, services, or products.

First e-Printing: June 2014
A product of in the United States of America
ISBN-13: 978-0-9858663-3-4

PLEASE NOTE: neither the author, Dennis Stapp, nor The Madison Institute Association have any vested interest that would constitute a conflict of interest in any of the companies or financial instruments mentioned in this book. This book is intended as a tool for the reader to investigate all possible investing options without being burdened with a 'sales pitch'.

Table of Contents

The Financial Fortress Plan

Keeping Your Money Safe During A Dollar Reset & Devaluation

By Dennis Stapp

For

THE MADISON INSTITUTE ASSOCIATION

<u>Introduction</u>

Many people are talking about an economic crash, and with good reason. Our crushing national debt has made it mathematically impossible to become solvent without the devaluation of the dollar. We see a dollar devaluation coming, and it will have the politically correct name of a 'dollar reset'. Just like a bank bail-out is now 'Quantitative Easing (QE)... it is just word spin for the same thing.

... and things are spiraling out of control.

In 2014 events sped up to destroy the US dollar: 1) Russia accelerated the St. Petersburg Exchange to price Russian oil/gas in rubles instead of dollars; 2) China and Russia agreed to trade oil/gas in only rubles and Yuan; 3) China is expected to announce all her oil/gas transactions will only be in Yuan: 4) the BRICS nations (Brazil, Russia, India, China, and South Africa) are creating international financial institutions in to challenge the International Monetary Fund (IMF) and World Bank (WBN); and 5) the IMF and WB, which meet only every 5 years, are expected to announce a replacement to the dollar world reserve currency in 2015 to deal with US dollar debt... they cannot wait another five years to deal with the world debt situation.

Additionally, on July 1, 2014 the Foreign Account Tax Compliance Act (FATCA) US statute comes into effect that requires all US persons, including individuals who live outside the United States, to report their financial accounts held outside of the United States, and requires foreign financial institutions to report to the Internal Revenue Service (IRS) about their American clients. Only one other country hunts down their citizens in foreign countries to tax them: the small African country of Eritrea. It is a law reminiscent of the legislation passed by Nazi leaders to strip the wealth of Jews trying to leave Germany prior to WWII.

Our US dollar financial system is under attack, and we are in trouble.

One of the most frequent questions asked at the Madison Institute Association's (TMI) meetings is: "how do I keep my money safe?" This puts us in an awkward situation because we have been tracking the crumbling economy for a number of years, know some of the pitfalls, but are surely not financial advisors. So we put the information out to the public as best we can, recommend that they seek advice from their financial advisor, and let them do with it as they wish.

Having said that, we feel that there are some data that we have uncovered that could be useful in making financial decisions. So we will put the following in the category of 'this is what we are considering'. To do this we must understand the situation we are in, the major players and what their objectives are, and how to keep our money safe when the elephants in the room stampede for the door.

PART ONE: THE ART OF GOING BROKE

First, we believe that the dollar collapse due to our wanton government spending is a surety. Hands down it will happen, but the 'when' part and other details are less well known. There is also unconfirmed information that at the most recent G20 meeting the discussion of devaluing the US dollar came up and was approved, accelerating the timeline; but more on that later.

Given all of that we must ask ourselves what does the term 'dollar crash' mean?

The dollar collapse means that the confidence of the dollar has dropped so low that people want to 'get out of the dollar' and there is an increasing glut of dollars that no one wants. It is a failure of the "full faith and credit of the dollar". This will be brought on by the interest on our debt growing to the point that our taxed output cannot keep up with the interest payments on our debt – let alone the payment of loan principal. It's like having a $100 per month paycheck and credit card minimum payment of $110; you're going broke. That is where we are.

So where does this money go? Well, it goes to a lot of places like congressional pork barrel programs, federally mandated social programs, successful lobbyists, military intervention into foreign lands to make sure that our 'economic interests' (read: the profit lines of multinational corporations based here in the United States) are 'protected', foreign aid to make other countries' societies more like us, defense department expenditures, and our huge 'black bag programs' budget that most of our congressmen cannot even see. We think it is fair to say that we need to have some serious discussions on what triggers military intervention and expenditures of tax monies in foreign countries. Our belief is that our money and blood need only be poured on foreign soil when absolutely necessary to protect our citizens. Protecting a corporation's business position for market share (when not a clear and present danger to the United States military, not energy, security) is not a good reason to have our sons and daughters come home in body bags.

And then there is the Great Casino in the Financial Sky – the derivatives market. The derivatives market is extremely complex, unregulated, and huge... very huge. In 2013 the notional size of the whole derivatives market was $1,200 Trillion dollars, while the global gross domestic product (GDP) was about $55 Trillion, and the United States GDP in the $14 Trillion range. It is literally a financial orgy of galactic scale created by non-producing financial parasites using other people's money. When people can produce money out of thin air things get very squirrely. When people create money out of thin air and are able to make bets on that money without any regulations – well, things go so insane as to be indescribable.

To put the financial casino into perspective (if you can); let's say you have a guy in New Mexico that makes a pack of rubber bands and sells it for a dollar. In the financial casino model there are bets totaling $22 that the single pack of rubber bands will go up in price, go down in price, will be swapped for paper clips, etc.

This lunacy is a product of our immoral financial system and it is ridiculous.

It actually doesn't work that way because the products are land, factories, financial loans, insurance policies, etc. that are packaged and repackaged over and over again, swapped and hedged until it becomes a financial monstrosity too large to comprehend. In fact there are no numbers on the size of the derivatives and the derivatives market because no one really knows, they are all just guesses. It's incomprehensibly large and all dependent on the world's reserve currency – The US fiat debt dollar (fiat= created out of nothing).

Now remember that the US dollar is a fiat debt note and is not backed by gold, so when you need more money than you have you print money out of thin air to cover your debt. We then package up the (more) debt that we created when we printed the money and sell the debt (as US Treasury bonds) that we promise to pay back with interest. All of this creates more debt, and makes our situation more impossible to repay back, and 'The Fed' resorts to printing more money. It's like trying to drink your-self sober. This is called 'monetizing the debt' – listen for that phrase the next time you watch the morning or nightly news.

OK, stay with me now, because this is where it gets interesting.

More dollars for the same amount of goods and services means that the dollar is worth less. It's like cutting a pie into 4 pieces or in 8 pieces. Only the foreigners that buy our debt buy a 1/4 piece of the pie and get 1/8 th back with a little interest. However, the interest isn't enough to make up the difference between a quarter and an eighth and the Chinese, Japanese, etc.; foreign investor actually loses buying power when his bond matures.

The foreign investors have gotten wise to this 'print your money out of thin air' and paying them back with cheap dollars scam, and aren't playing our debt bond game anymore. The recent US Bond auctions have seen a dramatic drop off in buyers for our bonds, so we have been printing up more money out of thin air to cover our debts. This is a modern day 'borrowing from Peter to pay Paul' situation.

This is the 'Quantitative Easing" (QE) that has been in the news lately; and now we are talking real big money: QE1 = $1.5 Trillion, QE2=$600 Billion, and QE3= $1.6 Trillion. The Fed was literally given a blank check book with a soft ceiling and no accountability for their actions; in fact these people (by law) cannot be sued for their actions. These laws were put into place by politicians accepting lots of money from banking concerns and related industry lobbyists. This is the disgusting legacy of our congressional 'representatives of the people'.

Also, don't forget that all of this debt is guaranteed to be ultimately paid by the US Taxpayer; you and me.

To put QE into perspective the 'Cash for Clunkers' program cost $3 Billion dollars, resulted in 690,114 dealer transactions, and went directly to the US citizen. It is debatable on the benefits of the program but the man on the street definitely did see an immediate tangible benefit. In contrast QE1 was supposed to go to US homeowners, but was shipped to foreign banks; after the first $100 billion went to the International Monetary Fund. When Bernanke was asked in congressional hearings where is the money, he said (and this is a direct quote from congressional hearings led by Congressman Alan Grayson from Florida): "I don't know". The QE series is 1,233 times larger; the bulk of the dollars went to banks overseas and none went directly to US homeowners... and we got stuck with the tab. With elected representation like this who needs a tyrant?

The short answer is that (resulting from legislative actions like the Gramm–Leach–Bliley Act) the US Federal Reserve (aka. 'The Fed') was given a credit card with no spending limits and a complicit congress with a penchant for buying votes through pet projects, social programs, congressional pay raises, and pork barrel spending. The QE series is a financial act of desperation, like a frenzied crack addict needing a 'fix' armed with a pocket full of credit cards that haven't expired yet. (No offense intended to crack addicts)

PART TWO: THE US DOLLAR COLLAPSES

So the actual collapse has started because countries realize that their hard earned Japanese Yen, Chinese Yuan, Brazilian Real, etc., that have been invested into US bond investments are not growing, but actually shrinking. They have begun to slow down the buying of US bonds; but countries like China cannot withdraw too quickly because to do so would tighten the US economy badly and cause the US to buy less Chinese imported goods. For their own trade interests they do not withdraw too fast.

This is the 'trade deficit' part of the problem. We printed up money (debt paper) to pay for out of control congressional spending, bundled it up into US treasury bonds, and sold the bonds at auction to (mostly) foreigners. We literally shipped our debt overseas in trade for goods like TVs, computers, microwave ovens, and cell phones.

People like the Chinese don't like the fact that their investments are tanking and that the US Dollar is nothing more than a kiss and a promise from Uncle Sam. They want, and deserve, some sort of assurances that they will not lose their money. As the Chinese threaten to pull out of the dollar for trade and bond buying, the US responds with assurances that the bonds are back by real collateral – the US owned government lands and natural resources. Yes, the massive debt that we have sold all over the world is ultimately backed by federal land collateral (mostly out west) that the US has 'bought' (confiscated by the Bureau of Land Management).

Not satisfied with the collateral arrangement, because they still had too many US Dollars, the Chinese started to buy up US properties like 1 Chase Manhattan Plaza. They realize that the future of the dollar is doomed and they will do anything to get out of the dollar without collapsing the world economy – for now.

The approach that China is taking is to convert all those US dollar debt based dollars into gold and real estate. The massive amount of excess dollars is being changed into gold, and deeds of US and other foreign property and energy resources like oil reserves.

The problem will come when the US dollar is devalued and becomes worthless. Then the Chinese will have to take ownership of the collateral, i.e., federal lands and resources that backed the debt bonds; but more on that later.

As bond buyers become scarcer the Federal Reserve buys the unbought bonds, and then they have to get rid of them. So where do they go? Many of the bonds are bought by the same institutional investors that make up the Central Banking Cartel called The Federal Reserve. Banks like J P Morgan, CitiBank, Bank of America buy up bonds to put into mutual funds that are sold to individual investors, smaller institutions, and pensions. They are sold as 'safe investments' because they are backed by the full faith and confidence of the US government; and they are insured by the FDIC.

We need to stop here for a moment and realize that very smart foreign institutional buyers and governments are running from dollars like a wet dog at a wedding. And these central bankers that created this debt are forced to take back the debt – and in turn are dumping it back on smaller investors, hidden in mutual funds and pensions. They do this because there is no one in congress exposing them and making them pay for their wrongdoing. They do this because they can.

I would suggest that you take a look at your own investments and see how much of your portfolio is in money market dollars, US bonds, and corporate bonds. These are the financial instruments that foreign investors like China, who are aware of the dollar's imminent demise, are running from.

As debt grows it feeds on itself. More debt causes the Fed to request more money to be printed from the Treasury, which in turn causes more debt. As debt spins out of control budget ceilings are broken, debt reporting is done by 'cooking the books' fraud, and the Fed resorts to wholesale printing of money in the form of Quantitative Easing.

As the debt death spiral grows the ability to pay off just the interest becomes an impossible task, and the holders of US debt paper become increasingly nervous that they will lose all of their invested money. This nervousness also feeds on itself. As nervous investors pull out of the dollar the remaining investors get more nervous and head for the exits.

This is where we are now, standing at the edge of the financial abyss. Big investors are sneaking out of the dollar while the masses watch news of Justin Bieber's latest arrest or Donald Sterling's struggles on TV.

At some point in time a seemingly small event comes out of nowhere and the debt balloon is burst and the elephants head for the exits. This will be pulling the trigger on the starting gun for the collapse. It is our belief that the government knows that we are at a point where a mass stampede to get out of the dollar is at hand. Let's face it, the government might be criminal, but they are not stupid on the risks or consequences of the collapse of their 'ponzi scheme'.

Not to get off point, but there are many smart economists and columnists that believe that the police build-up that we see on the streets of America is the preparation for a coming inevitable economic collapse. The theme goes like this: the economy is about to collapse, there is a protest or demonstration by concerned individuals that (by circumstances or planning) gets violent, the banks close down under the cover of chaos to devalue the dollar and blame it on the protestors, and the government steps in with force to keep a lid on the population as the economy is reset.

Regardless of how the situation goes down there will be a reset of the US dollar where the dollar will become worth a lot less in relation to other world currencies. This has to happen; all debts must be paid.

PART THREE: THE US DOLLAR RESETS

This is where it gets a little tricky. The US Dollar is currently the reserve currency for almost all international transactions. It is an outgrowth of the US and Saudi Arabian system to trade all Middle East oil in US Dollars. Countries who have money, resources, and little debt want to trade in something other than this dollar. The reason is that they have seen how debt ridden countries have failed in the past and do not want to fall victim to owning worthless dollars, or to suffer investing in a currency that depreciates over time. They want a stable trading currency that will not be subject to a possible crash or wealth shrinkage just because the transaction is executed in dollars. Eventually they want to replace the dollar, but they do not want to do it too quickly, which could cause the world economy to hopelessly crash in the process.

What seems to be the prevailing thought is that replacing the dollar will be a two-part process. First the US dollar will be 'split' into two virtual currencies, one international and one domestic based on the transaction they perform. It really will not be split per se; the exchange rate will be adjusted according to how the transaction unfolds. All transactions that are solely international in nature will be according to a new exchange rate of 3-5% less in value that is set by the G20 (or similar) body. This will divorce the reserve currency rate from the US dollar debt. In conjunction with the international dollar devaluation of 3-5%, all 'domestic dollar' purchases would be 'reset' to another, different, exchange rate. When buying foreign goods into the United States the 'domestic' dollar will be used at about 30-50% reduced exchange rate. I suspect that this will happen quickly, and there will have to be a bank 'holiday' to allow banks the time to change their accounting systems.

Let's say a person wants to by a $100 toaster from Walmart. Since it came from China the new price after the split would be $130-$150. The increase in price is the new international trade rate exchange. A $100 toaster that was manufactured in the US would still be $100 – but any of the parts and materials from overseas distributors would increase 30-35%. People overseas that plan to buy a $100 toaster manufactured wholly overseas with US dollars will now pay $103-$105. It's a simple concept of managing international dollar transactions differently than domestic transactions.

Portions of the actual exchange rate manipulation will be felt immediately, but the full impact of the 'reset' will take weeks to months to realize. This will be a result of the time that it takes for the goods and services providers to realize the higher cost of materials and energy, and the time it takes to pass it onto their consumer.

The second part of the process will be a physical replacement of the domestic dollar and / or the international US dollar. This will likely be a result of a campaign to say that old dollars must be traded in for new dollar. A new international dollar will likely be rolled out and the old US debt dollars will be sent back to America (in a vicious tidal wave of unwanted currency). Keeping the dollar as an international currency and printing a new domestic dollar is another (but unlikely) option to completing the process.

How the split actually plays out can be a couple of ways, but one thing is for sure – the US dollar will be divorced from the international reserve currency and the domestic dollar will drop to its true value as the 'full faith and credit'; of the US will be near zero.

What I have given you here is a most probable situation based on what we know.

The whole dollar exchange rate split choreography results in a Frankenstein system that is a temporary patch until international currency arrangements can be made under a new reserve currency to stabilize world trade. What an exchange rate split does is move all US debt back to its rightful owner (us) and functionally makes the US international dollar a temporary reserve currency outside of US domestic interests until it can be replaced by dominant regional currencies like the Yuan, a basket of currencies, a new gold backed international currency, or whatever.

Things are already moving in this direction. A little checking on the internet will show that some banks that have cross border checking account services outside the US already have language differentiating the 'US Dollar', and the 'International US Dollar'.

The end result for the US economy will be devastating. Everything that we buy from overseas will be drastically more expensive. US durable good spending will collapse, and it will be followed by massive factory closures. As a result the US will have to borrow debt paper to pay for goods, which means cranking up the printing presses in

Weimar fashion. This is where the US dollar will experience extreme hyperinflation. Based on the amount of debt we have outstanding, already collateralized land resources, and the lack of tangible manufacturing we have – we suspect that US hyperinflation will rival, and possibly exceed, the Weimar Republic and Zimbabwe.

But it will not exactly be an instantaneous hyperinflationary situation per se. Temporarily prices of all necessities will skyrocket, while prices for luxury items and cars will drop like a rock. As soon as things start to settle out foreign buyers will scoop up deals on houses, cars, land, factories, etc. as the impoverished American seeks to pay for imported necessities.

PART FOUR: YOUR PORTFOLIO

If we take a look at these events and what is unfolding we see that the dollar will have little to no value, but what will the new rates be like? How will the rates be created?

The new exchange rate will be calculated by some international body like the G20 – you know, those unelected bankers posing as heads of state that have no accountability to the US Congress, the US Citizen, nor any citizens of any nation. Remember that the G8 was expanded to the G20 in 2008 during the US economic 'recession' when they found out that the G8 had only one member (Russia) that had any semblance of being solvent – the rest were broke or going broke. They gladly added countries that actually had money like Brazil, India, China, and South Africa (plus Russia makes the 'BRICS' members).

However, the borrower is slave to the lender and the BRICS members are now the 'lenders' calling the shots.

It needs to be noted here that the introduction of a new reserve currency will have catastrophic consequences not only on the US but other countries that are neck deep in debt, have few resources, and are at risk of not paying their debts. What immediately comes to mind are the United Kingdom, Japan, and the PIIGS (Portugal, Italy, Ireland, Greece and Spain). These are countries that are (almost) hopelessly in debt. Any financial defense plan should stay away from investing in these nations.

So, the BRICS want to have the new international reserve currency backed by something more than just a kiss and a promise from Uncle Sam and a hug from the House of Saud. They want a currency that is stable; something with tangible backing. The new world reserve currency needs to have real value; and the exchange rates of each country's currency needs to accurately reflect that country's debt and ability to pay that debt.

Let's look at Brazil as an example. Brazil has money, resources, little debt, and wants to do business with other countries in an honest way. They need an international currency to do business, and this international reserve currency needs to have exchange rates set for all countries of the world. They do not want to exchange their national currency (the Brazilian Real), that has no debt, for a US Dollar that is hopelessly in debt and will crash (become worth less) at some time in the future. If the US dollar does crash, the Brazilians need to be assured that the US can pay off their debts. However, the US has shipped much of its manufacturing overseas, and used its land and resources as loan collateral. So, the Brazilian point of view is that the US dollar should be worth a lot less than the Brazilian Real.

And the Brazilians are right.

So in the coming months we will see the devaluation of the US Dollar with respect to the Brazilian Real when the US Dollar buys Brazilian goods. By extension we will see this principle used when the new reserve currency is rolled out and the US Dollar value is reset to whatever is used as the new reserve currency – temporary or otherwise.

Now that we understand how things work we can start making some decisions on how to keep our money safe (maybe).

First of all you need to understand that anything that is based on the US Dollar will be trampled to death in the near future. Let's take a look at some of the things we are talking about [This is not complete, but it will give you an idea on how things will unfold.]:

- **Stocks:** The US stock market is a US Dollar based casino that is corrupt and rigged as bad, or worse, than the mobster controlled gambling houses of Las Vegas past (no offense to the mobsters of the Las Vegas past). Companies like Hewlett Packard, Verizon, GE, Boeing, McKesson, WalMart, Costco, etc., will have their domestic US businesses and money reserves 'shrunk' by 30-50%; and consequently their management will have to cut corners, staff, services, and increase profits in an effort to survive – if they can. All costs of foreign materials and services will skyrocket as everyone in their supply chain will be forced to raise costs due to devaluation, and then raise costs because other suppliers have raised costs. The interconnectivity of large companies and the synergy of increasing costs causing increasing costs will assure a domino effect through the stock market. Once it starts it will be very difficult to regain enough confidence to stop a slide, but many people will ride their investments to the bottom in the hopes that the market will turn around. The exceptions are foreign owned gold, silver, oil, and food stocks that should do well in a dollar contracting market.
- **US Money Market Mutual Funds:** if you are invested in US money market mutual fund(s) then you are betting directly on the stability of a dollar that is in a

lot of trouble. Your investments will take a severe hit with any devaluation of the dollar. With a devaluation of the US Dollar comes loss of confidence in the dollar, more risk, and less purchasing power.

- **US Money Market Deposit Accounts**: Unlike the Money Market Mutual Funds, Money Market Accounts are insured by the FDIC, but I wouldn't take much comfort in that. The FDIC (as of April 2013) only held about $25 Billion to cover some $9,300 Billion in US Deposit assets. If the FDIC does have to dig deep into its pockets to bail out depositors and they hit the bottom then they will crank up the printing presses and pay you back in funny money; but it isn't funny anymore because it will be worth less if / when you get it.

- **US Treasury Bonds**: These are straight dollar denominated IOUs issued by the US Treasury and could be the hardest hit financial instrument by devaluation. Just think that many Chinese money managers and lot of smart guys in other countries are dumping US Treasury Bonds like a drunken prom date. Why would you want to invest in the hope that they will appreciate?

- **State Municipal Bonds**: The situation of state/county/local bonds is abysmal to frightening. Municipalities like Detroit, San Bernardino (CA), Harrisburg (PA), and Jefferson county Alabama are just some of the places that are hopelessly bankrupt.

In 2010 there were 38 municipalities and 8 general purpose local government bankruptcy filings – and that is in good times. What do you think will happen when the dollar is devalued and hard time really hit? Our opinion is pretty clear that state, count, and local bonds are unwise investments because they: 1) depend on dollar denominated financial instruments, and 2) the bonds are generally in business interests that will suffer greatly when the dollar devaluation hits. When the devaluation comes borrowers will get a three punch combination where the basic dollar will shrink in purchasing power, all peripheral prices for support activities will inflate, and the borrower will face increasing material and labor costs that will make it next to impossible to pay back.

- **Bank Deposits:** It may come as a shock to you, but when you deposit money into a bank account you no longer 'own' the money; you become an unsecured creditor holding a bank IOU, and have no legal rights to your money beyond that IOU that has no collateral behind it. You see banks want collateral when they loan money, but when you loan them money you get nothing for collateral; but you do get the false assurances of a bankrupt FDIC.

Instead of a kiss and a promise from Uncle Sam when you buy bonds, you are now making out with your local banker when you deposit your money with them. Let me explain.

The 'rules' for what happens when your bank defaults are contained in a joint international 2012 FDIC-BOE (Bank of England) report titled: <u>Resolving Globally Active, Systematically Important Financial Institutions.</u> The report states that in a time of crisis the bank depositor (that would be you) would have his/her money converted (that would be confiscated and transformed) into 'bank equity' (that would be stock in the bank you have your deposits) and there are 'no exceptions' for 'insured deposits' (that means any deposits that you think are guaranteed by the FDIC are not. Translating it into plain language: FDIC insurance means nothing and does not apply under these circumstances). So you have it there. In a situation like what we are talking about where the dollar is devalued there will be plenty of banks in severe distress and failing. The bank 'holiday' means that the rat trap has snapped shut and you will not be able to get your money out of the bank – no way, no how. When your large bank opens up you will be the proud owner of bank stock shares in a failing bank dealing in a currency that no one on the planet wants, at a time when no one can (or wants to) lend anyone any money.

- **<u>Real Estate</u>:** This is also a bad investment, but for some different reasons. In a dollar devalued economy no one will want to loan money and no one will have the money to buy a home (or other real estate for that matter). As the economy gets tighter mortgage companies will need to cut spending and raise cash to cover their bills. So they will increasingly execute the acceleration clause within your mortgage contract that demands near immediate payment of the loan in full; which will make the overall situation much worse. There usually is a trigger, like late payments, but after talking to an attorney on this we find out that the ability to execute the acceleration clause usually has loopholes enough that cover just about any economic situation. A massive economic upheaval, like the one we are talking about, will cause a sharp upswing in unemployment and give cause for the bank to demand mortgage payment immediately under these 'scared lender' clauses.

Regardless, an economic crash of this nature will cause a glut of homes to be up for sale and a surge in unemployment. Banks will be going under and people will be going broke. The housing market will be crushed and there will be a mass exodus from home ownership to rental accommodations as people liquidate any equity they have to survive. In response to demand and rising inflationary costs, rents will skyrocket. Then the government will step in and put a cap on rental payments. Landlords who live on cash flow and do not own the rental property outright will likely lose their properties. People who do own rental property that is paid off will raise rents as high as they can to keep up with the rising costs of everything else. Some will take the opportunity to gouge people on rent and likely be sued. As inflation soars the squeeze between rising costs and rent ceilings will put many landlords owning their property out of business.

This is not pure speculation because this is what happened in the crash of 1929. By all accounts this devaluation will be more severe, and we suspect that the same things will happen – only worse.

- **Pensions / Retirement Funds:** Sadly, this is where things get very ugly in a personal way. Many pensions are unfunded or underfunded, which leaves them at risk. The vast majority of the pension funds invest in the above financial areas that will be crushed in a dollar devaluation collapse. However, it seems to be one of the last storehouses of 'wealth' in these United States; and a broke and desperate government will come hunting for any money it can lay its hands on.

We firmly believe that the government will 'nationalize' all pensions and retirement funds in this collapse. What this means is that the government will confiscate all of your funds and convert them into US Treasury Bond IOUs. These will be the same bonds that everyone on the planet will be dumping and trying to get away from. The government will confiscate your pension to pay bills and promise to pay you back with worthless bonds. Anyone who is counting on their retirement fund to support them now, or in the near future, should take a look at how it is invested and compare it to the list of investments above.

The combination of job loss, home loss, and pension loss will devastate the remaining 'Great Generation' and their sons and daughters. This will be the most heart wrenching tragedy that results from the folly of our out of control, socialistic, European wannabe, 'globalist' government. The loss of property, freedom, and peace of mind is the price we will pay – dearly- for sitting on our asses while corrupt politicians ruined this nation.

- **Taxes:** Our government will be like a crazed animal flailing to gain its balance, and nothing will seem to work. They will need money, lots of money, to keep their government running and programs going – so they will raise taxes with a vengeance. Expect current taxes to be raised on everything, new taxes to be created, and things that have not been taxed before will be taxed. One thing that we think will be assured is a 'means' tax. What that entails is a tax on how 'rich' you are. Your total net worth of cars, home, jewelry, cottage, business, savings, etc., will be added up and a portion of that total will be taxed – and you will be expected to pay that under threat of prosecution. Everything that you paid taxes on will be taxed again. As you pay these taxes and get less rich your taxes will start to go down, but it will be a 'starvation-diet' death where asset wealth will be slowly bled off until the crisis is over, or until you join the ranks of the poor.

- **<u>Precious Metals Mining Stocks</u>:** Our view of the whole economy relative to mining stocks shows that precious metals prices have been deliberately suppressed so that the central bankers can continue their fiat 'money' scheme. If the price of gold were to be realized for what it is (i.e., much higher in terms of fiat dollars), then the US dollar would be exposed for what it is – nothing but a debt IOU with a shaky prospect of repayment.

When you take that into account US precious metals mining stocks may be the best investment on the stock exchange. Right now many mining concerns are barely making profits and some have actually stopped or slowed mining operations because the cost to mine is being squeezed by the suppressed price per ounce of gold, and profits are way down. We expect that mining stocks will rise significantly as BRICS nations demand that international currencies be backed by more than just IOUs. This is validated by the quiet panic for China to get its hands on as much gold as possible. Also, demand for gold jewelry and coins in China and India is way up.

We expect stocks will move, and then the dollar will split; but resist "shorting" the market. This is risky and a stategy only for seasoned traders. Better to consider re-structuring directly into foreign precious metals and energy stocks like Silver Wheaton Corp. (gold/silver), First Majestic Silver of Mexico, and Suncor Energy (oil). These type stocks have products that are in demand in tight economies and stock prices that are expected to be revalued according to the exchange rate of the parent country.

- **<u>Gold / Silver Certificates</u>:** Unlike the precious metals stocks, precious metals certificates need to be avoided. A gold or silver certificate is supposed to be a 'title deed' to a gold or silver bar kept in your name in a vault somewhere. The certificate will likely state the name of the custodian, location of the vault that the bar resides, bar number (unique identifying number), etc.; however, there are problems here.

Vaults are run by people with bankers mentality; and bankers make a nice profit out of fractional banking (the process of loaning out more money than the bankers have in the hopes that they will have enough on hand to service withdrawals). In the banking world fractional banking is may not be moral, but it is legal (no one ever said our laws have to be moral, which is one reason why we are in such a mess as a country). In the world of precious metals certificates 'fractional banking' is highly illegal. The certificate that you have that says a certain bar located at a vault id owned by you and only you – might not be legitimate.

There is a lot of information pointing to widespread fraud in the precious metals certificate business, and this author has spoken directly with a broker that had his clients gold sold many times over (if my memory serves me well I think that it was over a dozen). Also, some economists have calculated that the total gold weight represented by the total number of certificates is more than the estimated mined global reserves.

It is for these reasons that I would stay away from gold / silver certificates. Something fishy is going on there and I wouldn't want anyone to wind up being scammed out of their hard earned money.

- **Gold / Silver**: This is an interesting situation because historically gold and silver are places to run to when currencies start to stink like a dead fish in the noon day sun. We believe that the price per ounce of gold is being fraudulently manipulated by banking interests that want to keep the dollar Ponzi scheme going. We also think that it is being done as the worst kept open secret as a result of our regulatory agencies willfully turning a blind eye to the wrongdoing. Remember that in the incestuous banking business many of the 'regulators' are former Goldman-Sachs, JP Morgan, etc., executives. They know how to play the game because they ARE the game.

  We believe that the price of gold and silver will sky rocket and whatever new international reserve currency results from this economic spasmodic episode will have gold as a major commodity component. However, we are not unified in thinking how the government will treat gold once the devaluation starts. Some think that the US will not confiscate gold from its citizens because to do so would incur the wrath of an already angry public to the point that there could be violence against government and banking officials. Their thinking is that if violence hasn't been realized after devaluation, bank confiscations, pension looting, and massive foreclosures, then confiscation of gold is akin to gun grabs and will put many over the top. It's the old saying that you don't touch a man's God, guns, or gold. If gold is confiscated it will be "bought" at depressed prices; i.e., swapped for US inflated debt paper that will increasingly drop towards zero. After the government gets your gold you can expect that the price per ounce of gold will go up dramatically. That is what this government did the last time it confiscated gold. It was theft of personal property value by a government scam that was made legal by congress.

I think that you get the picture by now. The game that the government will be playing is to grab everything that represents real wealth and trade it for debt paper printed out of thin air. What they cannot confiscate they will tax to the point of destruction. Their objective is to liquidate their debt (created by congress and the non-producing financial parasites) by taking or taxing your savings, pensions, home, and future earnings.

It's a tough call whether or not to hold physical gold or silver. On one hand the rampant fraud in the gold market would suggest that you consider only owning physical gold that has been tested true. Counterfeit US gold bars have turned up in Germany and China, and it is widely believed (with reason) that many of the gold certificates that claim ownership of individual bars with serial numbers have actually been sold many times over. On the other hand you run the risk of the US government issuing an order to confiscate gold. There is no clear answer here. All we can do is try to present the facts.

So many the above financial instruments are about as toxic as you can get in a dollar devaluation situation. You probably noticed that the cards are stacked against the US citizen; and favor the banks, financial institutions, and government. This is all compliments of our representatives in Washington DC. Big money can afford many trips to congressional offices to deliver expensive and slick lobby presentations, and skew legislation in favor of those banks and corporations that have the big dollars. Over time you get where we are. The greediest banks and corporations gain the most leverage against the common man. The man on the street becomes the object of these sharks to have his pocket picked, and have the cards stacked against him in any legal matter. So much for our representatives, who are looking out for our best interests?

Part Five: Actions for Financial Self Defense

Finally, we are here; where the rubber meets the road.

Now that we have explained the problems we have, how we think events will unfold, and presented a litany of what investment not to have... the big question becomes: "Where do I put my money to try to keep it safe?" We say 'try' because we have to remember that the places that we can put money are being controlled by the very people who created this mess in the first place. They can change their mind at any time, get legislation passed to change the rules, and they could play the "I'll take your money from you and you can sue me to try to get it back" game. In that case you are up against a well-funded and powerful government that has appointed the very judge that will hear the trial. Also remember that this information is just for educational purposes and any action or inaction taken by the reader is the sole responsibility of him/her and their financial advisor.

The basics are simple: take your money from the risky areas and put it into less risky areas. In this case you would want to take your money from dollar denominated investments, and investments affected by a dollar devaluation episode and put them into investments that will appreciate with respect to the dollar and (hopefully) will be out of the reach of US government confiscation and taxation.

To this end you need to seriously think about reviewing your investments and seeing if they are rooted in dollar debt paper. If you have mutual funds you need to know where those mutual funds put your money. Check the prospectus. It should tell you if you are putting you money in US Treasury Bonds, Real Estate Investments, Corporate bonds, Municipal bonds, domestic stocks, money markets, etc. all of which would turn very toxic in the event of a dollar devaluation. Go through the list of above devaluation risky 'investments', and do your research to get out of dollar debt based investments.

So where would you want to put your money?

Banks:

First let's take a look at your bank. Banks don't make anything, they are not manufacturing companies. They are the experts in taking risks with other people's money to make more money – and please note that is what got us into this situation in the first place. However, I have to say that ethical and moral banks have their place in society; it's just when they run wild that disaster can happen. What we need to do is to find good banks that have solid balance sheets that will resist default in the case of a collapsing economy.

The best place we have found for data on bank strength and weakness is Martin Weiss's data on bank strength. He seems to do an excellent job at objectively scoring financial institutions, and we would recommend that you take a serious look at your bank and how it stacks up to other banks in your area. He lists banks by name from

Bank	City	State	Total Assets ($000)	Weiss Financial Strength Rating
First National Bank Alaska	Anchorage	AK	$2,651,980	B+
Mount McKinley Bank	Fairbanks	AK	$282,850	A-
Bank of Brewton	Brewton	AL	$57,650	A-
Bank of York	York	AL	$78,090	B+
BankSouth	Dothan	AL	$232,130	A-
Brantley Bank & Trust Company	Brantley	AL	$63,670	B+
Central State Bank	Calera	AL	$153,560	B+
Citizens Bank	Geneva	AL	$161,360	A
Citizens Bank	Greensboro	AL	$86,390	A-
Citizens Bank of Winfield	Winfield	AL	$205,600	A
Farmers & Merchants Bank	Waterloo	AL	$61,210	A
Farmers & Merchants Bank	LaFayette	AL	$102,350	A-
First Bank of Boaz	Boaz	AL	$164,120	A
First Metro Bank	Muscle Shoals	AL	$418,940	A-
First National Bank	Hamilton	AL	$271,720	A-
First National Bank of Talladega	Talladega	AL	$386,670	A
Liberty Bank	Geraldine	AL	$99,330	A-
Peoples Southern Bank	Clanton	AL	$141,130	A-
Phenix-Girard Bank	Phenix City	AL	$142,000	B+
Robertson Banking Company	Demopolis	AL	$236,310	B+
Samson Banking Company	Samson	AL	$53,310	A-
State Bank & Trust	Winfield	AL	$180,660	A

worst to best and gives them an alphabet grade rating, just like in grade school. Here are examples of the best and worst bank and thrifts according to Weiss:

Bank	City	State	Total Assets ($000)	Weiss Financial Strength Rating
Alaska Pacific Bank	Juneau	AK	$179,085	D
Alabama Trust Bank, National Association	Sylacauga	AL	$71,650	D-
Aliant Bank	Alexander City	AL	$980,770	D-
Bank of Evergreen	Evergreen	AL	$49,830	D+
Bank of Tuscaloosa	Tuscaloosa	AL	$511,210	D+
Bank of Vernon	Vernon	AL	$187,170	D-
BankTrust	Mobile	AL	$1,942,850	D-
Bay Bank	Mobile	AL	$89,960	D-
Bryant Bank	Tuscaloosa	AL	$831,060	D
CB&S Bank	Russellville	AL	$1,353,640	D
Citizens Bank	Enterprise	AL	$95,200	D+
Citizens' Bank, Inc.	Robertsdale	AL	$111,840	D
Community Bank & Trust-Alabama	Union Springs	AL	$104,230	E
Community Bank & Trust of Southeast Alabama	Dothan	AL	$539,290	D+
Compass Bank	Birmingham	AL	$64,611,560	D-
Escambia County Bank	Flomaton	AL	$96,290	D
EvaBank	Cullman	AL	$419,490	E-
Exchange Bank of Alabama	Altoona	AL	$246,580	D
Farmers Exchange Bank	Louisville	AL	$193,110	D-
First Bank of the South	Rainsville	AL	$81,760	D
First Commercial Bank	Birmingham	AL	$1,985,420	D
First Federal Bank, A Federal Savings Bank	Tuscaloosa	AL	$157,437	D+
First Financial Bank	Bessemer	AL	$223,080	D-

Your banking money should be treated differently than your investment money. We would suggest that you consider moving your money from the weaker banks to the stronger banks. This should be where you store your cash from your checking account and a place to manage cash flow; it is not the place you want to put your investment dollars. Making this move will not protect you from the dollar devaluation, but it just might protect you from having the bulk of your money in a bank that defaults and leaves you stuck with stock shares in a bankrupt bank. Regardless, it is always a good idea to do business with a bank that is strong financially and not weak.

Now that we have gotten some of your dollars secured in 'good' banks, we need to turn our attention to the rest of your wealth. The bulk of your money isn't likely to be in a checking account – and it shouldn't be. It needs to be in a place where it can quietly make money with as little risk as possible. To protect your wealth from a US dollar devalue attack you need to make sure that your wealth isn't rooted in US dollars; for if they are then your whole investment strategy is at risk. Remember the analogy that if you own two pieces of pie one day and devaluation comes along, then you still have two pieces of pie, but all of the pieces are a lot smaller – and your family is a lot hungrier.

Bank Safe Deposit Boxes

Bank safe deposit boxes are safe from everyone except the bank and the government; or put another way: they are safe from unauthorized thieves. Just remember that you will be putting your valuables in a box that is totally controlled by a banking system and government that is hopelessly broke and in a panic to grab anything of value to survive. Overall, putting your valuables in their hands is a very questionable strategy.

In a dollar reset scenario there is likely to be a bank holiday when the banks can re-tool their software and policies to align with new government dictates. Bank safe deposit boxes are subject to 'bank holiday' closures and you will not be able to get your valuables out – no matter how hard you try. These safe deposit boxes are subject to any bank regulations; and a bank holiday is only one regulation. You can expect a number of new laws and regulations to be passed as the banks restructure, and expect that you will only be able to access those valuables that meet the new regulations.

Right now your Safe Deposit box is also subject to an IRS freeze or seizure. If the IRS suspects that you have something of value and you have been crushed into poverty by the dollar devaluation; then it is reasonable to expect that the IRS could seize your safe deposit box under the excuse that they would not want you to run off with unreported valuables – so let's just seize them before you have an opportunity to take them away, and we (the IRS) will give them back to you if we feel that they are not subject to a new tax law.

The bottom line is that there are downsides to a bank safe deposit box. You might be better off by buying a large safe and bolting it down in your home. Looting might be an issue if you live in a larger city, but in most places you can at least pull a gun on a would-be robber to protect your valuables. So you need to think whether your valuables are at risk by common thieves, or by authorized thieves – it's your choice; the difference is that you can legally shoot unauthorized thieves if you catch them in the act.

Foreign Investments

So we need to get out of the US dollar. There are two predominant thoughts on this: 1) foreign investments; and 2) gold and silver. Let's take a look at both of these.

The first thing to consider is some sort of foreign investment; but not just any foreign investment. All countries are not the same. Some have more debt, less resources, and less stable governments. These are the general rules: 1) less debt =good / more debt = bad; 2) more natural resources = good / less natural resources = bad; 3) gold backed currency = good / debt based currency = bad; 4) more gold owned by the country = good / less gold owned by the country = bad; stable government = good / unstable government = bad.

Lenders (and that is what you are when you 'invest' in a financial instrument) that are smart only lend money to borrowers that are financially able to pay back the money. That rules out the US, Japan, Europe, UK, etc. These countries are awash in debt and are up to their eyeballs in derivative casino debt.

So what we are looking for is a place to put our savings where that country isn't up to its neck in debt, has a lot of natural resources, has a gold backed currency, has a lot of gold, and the government is stable. When you start to boil these countries down what immediately pops up are the BRICS (Brazil, Russia, India, China, and South Africa) nations. They are widely recognized by economists as more likely to come out on the good side of any demise of the dollar as the reserve currency. You can find more information on national debt by country at Wikipedia.

The reason that someone would want to invest in the BRICS countries is that when the US International dollar is re-valued it will be re-valued relative to other currencies. The term 'revalued relative to other currencies' mean that (roughly) the exchange rate will be adjusted according to each nations productive output, energy availability and consumption, gold reserves, and its ability to repay loans. Take China for instance. It has a lot of production capability, has oil and gas contracts in place with the Middle East and Russia, has substantial gold reserves and has a very good ability to repay its debts. [Ed Note: contrary to 'common knowledge' and the figure reported by the World Gold Council that China has only 1054 metric tonnes, we firmly believe that this number is woefully low, and is more than twice this number.]

Foreign Bonds

What we would want is a BRICS government guaranteed bond or Certificate of Deposit (CD) that is backed by the full faith and credit of one of the financially strongest nations on the planet. An example of one strategy would be to buy a BRICS bond that would mature over some short time that is long enough to ride out the dollar devaluation and settling down of a new world reserve currency.

If you do invest in a foreign government bond you will have to pay gains taxes on it once it matures or is withdrawn. The Federal Reserve banking cartel and the US IRS want 'their' money and will use all manner of IRS warrants and confiscation measures to get it away from you. Remember that you will be parking your money out of harm's way to avoid devaluation, letting the International Dollar Investment appreciate, and then possibly 'cashing in' at a time when the US is looking for any reason to take as much money as they can to pay their bills. Although the taxes are expected to be nontrivial, the appreciation in a BRICS invested account should easily offset the taxes enough that you would expect a relatively sizeable profit.

An issue with this strategy is that it is difficult for us mere mortals to invest in safe financial instruments like this. Stock brokers are under a great deal of pressure to generate stock sales; and the investment house is a trader of stocks also. Think of it this way. Why should a stock investment house sell an up and coming stock to its clients before buying it themselves? If the stock house buys it first and then 'pushes it' to their clients, then those clients who buy will help push the stock (and their profits) up. What you have is a system ripe for abuse... from conflicts of interest in recommending their favored stocks that they are recommending ('pushing'), to outright 'pump and dump' illegal activities. Although large investment houses do invest in foreign government debt – particularly in countries that are not on the 'going broke' train – these investment houses do not have any incentive to share this strategy with the little investor; it's just not a money maker for them.

Everyone on the planet knows that the mature industrialized nations are drowning in debt and that the BRICS nations are not only debt stable, they have a lot of resources and manufacturing capability for the future. So why is it when I 'Google' BRICS bond and CD investments I come up with nothing? You would think that investment houses would be on the financial bandwagon moving client's money from debt ridden countries to the safer countries with a prosperous future – and they are doing it; just not for you.

Regardless there are some ethical investment houses out there, and it would be smart to ask your financial advisor about investing in BRICS government bonds or CDs.

Investing in Foreign Currency CDs

One thing that could save you from financial ruin is investing in foreign currency CDs. There is one place that I know of that actually has foreign currency investment CDs. It is an online banking concern called Everbank.com. The rates of return are small, usually in the single digit percentage, but they would keep you safe from a 30% devaluation drop. A 2% increase coupled with a 30% gives you as relative 'increase' of 32% over a flat-lined devalued dollar investment. The CDs are offered in 'baskets' of currencies with different investment strategies. I would favor the Global Power Shift® commodity rich CD, or the Balanced Debt SM economy driven basket. Both of these CDs seem to have good fundamentals when considering a dollar devaluation scenario.

Once again the strategy would be to park investment monies in these CDs in times of high devaluation risk, and roll them over into the same until the risk has passed. Once the risk is passed you can put them into other financial instruments; like whatever the next world reserve currency would be.

Gold and Silver

When global power is shifting it is best to watch what the big dogs are doing to see where it is best to put money. Right now the high stakes players are getting out of the dollar, investing in countries that are financially solvent and have great potential in the 'post-devaluation' economy, and they are investing in gold. China, Russia, and India are into gold in a big way; with China leading the buying frenzy pack. Like I said before, we believe the Chinese have more than 2700 metric tonnes of gold rather than the 1054 tonnes reported to the World Gold Council. On top of that China has been rumored to be buying gold through a Singapore front; which increases her overall reserves.

However, the craftiest thing that the Chinese have done is to encourage (with great zeal) the Chinese public to buy as much gold as they can. Private gold can be confiscated by Chinese communist government to reach the rumored 6000 tonne goal that would make China a legitimate contender for the world's reserve currency. There is a real argument that China is making a run at the world's reserve currency and using gold as the vehicle. If so, smart investors should look hard at owning physical gold.

Many are concerned about having their gold confiscated, and this is a controversial topic. Public ownership of gold in China and the post devaluation US government taxing everything of value to 'get out of debt' tends to support the gold confiscation argument; but in the 1929 depression less than 5% of private gold was turned in. A more probable situation is where the government controls the price of gold and allows it to increase only a small percentage per day or week. Limiting the expanse of gold only slows the price rise – it will eventually find its true value.

Regardless, we are in favor of personal ownership of gold as a hedge on hard times; but we need to look at a couple more risks and investment possibilities before we exit gold as a defense strategy.

Not long ago a German gold refinery bought some gold bars that turned out to be counterfeit, they had tungsten cores and not gold. The bars were marked US with US ID numbers. Shortly afterwards the Chinese received some of the same type bars, also with US markings.

Two things resulted from this: 1) The Chinese took all bars incoming into their gold reserves, and re-melted them down and recast them with Chinese markings; exposing any counterfeit bars. 2) The Germans demanded that their gold bars (that are supposed to be) held in the New York vault be returned. However, a funny thing happened. The US said that they would get their bars back, but it would take seven years to return the bars. That startling revelation caused Germany to demand its gold back from France and Switzerland to demand their gold back from the US.

Something stinks here.

Needless to say, if you buy physical gold, make sure that you are getting gold and not getting scammed. But what about paper 'deed' to gold? Sorry to say that this situation is even worse. The amount of (rumored, but well documented) fraud in the gold trade industry is legendary. There are reports of bars of gold that are supposed to be unique and sold only once, but are sold many times over; which is strictly illegal. This is a subject that is long and is beyond the scope of this article, but the reader is urged to go to the Gold Anti-Trust Action Committee website to review the current legal actions to exposed and litigate against people involved in gold fraud. But all is not lost for owning physical gold.

BullionVault seems to be a reputable company in the gold storage service business. It allows you to buy and store gold and silver outside the US and denominate it in the host countries currency. You can buy and store gold and silver in Switzerland, London, New York, Toronto, or Singapore. There is a service charge and putting your wealth in one of these vaults will not return interest payments. The attraction in this 'investment' is that gold and silver have intrinsic stored wealth, whereas fiat US debt dollar, or any debt dollar for that matter, does not. A devaluation of 30% will immediately cause gold to go up 30% to account for the devaluation, but it will also likely appreciate due to demand of individuals, institutions, and nations wanting to flee from a falling currency and seek the refuge that gold and silver has to offer.

It is our belief that gold and silver have been illegally, systematically, and brutally suppressed in price, and when the devaluation comes, gold and silver will be extremely attractive as an investment.

Directly Investing in Chinese Yuan

[Please note that the Renminbi is the official name for the Chinese currency, and Yuan is the main unit of currency. For the sake of simplicity this report will use the term 'Yuan' exclusively and interchangeably.]

By all accounts China seems to be the leading world power in planning and preparation for the post-apocalyptic economy. China is or has: 1) been moving away from the US dollar and is resisting buying any new US debt; 2) has entered into multi-year agreements with Russia and Iran for oil and gas; 3) has enticed manufacturing from the US and Europe in a way that builds their manufacturing infrastructure, strengthens their research and development capability, and increases their access to patents and intellectual property; 4) is buying gold through third party agents in a way that does not increase the spot cost of gold, but can be put into Chinese coffers when the time is right; 5) has made military buildup a national priority; 6)made moves to unify the BRICS nations to rival, and to eventually supplant the IMF and the World Bank; and 7) has been quietly buying up US Federal Reserve with the assistance of Spanish and German banks (see Dave Hodge : World war III Has Already Been Lost):

"It would be appropriate to think of this development as the United States government doing a debt consolidation of all its treasury bonds because it can no longer pay or service the debt and the Chinese and their partners are acquiring the assets of America for pennies on the dollar. It will soon be announced that China is in the process of purchasing major Western banks (e.g. Bank of America, Wells Fargo) and physical assets. These banks make up the majority owners of the Federal Reserve. By purchasing these banks as distressed properties, the Chinese, will in effect; have purchased the Federal Reserve because these banks own the Federal Reserve."

If you think that China is going to be the big dog on the block after the dollar crashes, then it would make sense that you would consider investing directly in the Chinese Yuan. In David Hodge's article mentioned above he estimates that the dollar will be devalued at a 6:1 ratio where it will take 6 times the number of dollars to buy the same Chinese goods as today.

As an example if you bought a generator from China today for $500; then after the dollar 'reset' the 6:1 exchange rate would make it cost $3000. There is some logic to this as the Yuan is about 16 cents per dollar; and to keep a semblance of a Yuan based reserve currency would yield an exchange rate of 6:1.

Please note that in my example on splitting the dollar I use a 30-50% drop in the domestic dollar, and in David Hodges article he assumes an 84% drop (6:1 ratio exchange rate). I think that both of these could be plausible. The articles I have read indicate that the G20 is looking at INITIALLY dropping the dollar by 30-50%; where as Mr. Hodges looks at the ULTIMATE drop of 84%. If you assume that things will ripple through the economy and get worse before they get better, then a drop of 84% is certainly possible.

OK, you decide that China will be the 'winner' once the dollar devaluation is complete – then how do you get on the 'winning' side? Before you do you need to know that most (all?) of the investment instrument that are Yuan based are not FDIC insured and the Yuan is a 'floating' currency; which means that the value can go up or down, However, if you have been paying attention to the information in this article that should not stop you from investing (see the disclaimer at the beginning of this report).

First you could invest directly in the Yuan (Renminbi) through Everbank's <u>WorldCurrency Access® Deposit Account.</u> It is essentially a money market account that uses the Chinese Yuan as its base product instead of the dollar. What is nice about this instrument is that the minimum to open an account is only $2500.

Secondly, you could choose Everbank's <u>Chinese Renminbi Non-Deliverable Fund</u>. This will give you access to investing in the Yuan (Renminbi); but note that this is a non-deliverable fund, which means that you cannot take delivery of the foreign currency, but can take advantage of any favorable exchange rate changes. That is, in a 6:1 exchange rate scenario you will get back six times the dollars that you put in when cashing out of the account (all other things being equal).

Please note that there are other currency options that are offered by Everbank, and other currencies can be selected. The main point here is to try to select a currency that is more solvent than the US dollar (less national debt), politically stable, has abundant natural resources, and has good labor / manufacturing fundamentals.

Also, you could invest in an exchange traded fund (ETF) like the Wisdom Tree Dreyfus Chinese Yuan ETF (NYSE: CYB). This is pegged to the currency itself, and is much like the Everbank. The Bank of China sets the rate based on that basket each day. The Yuan (Renminbi) is a highly manipulated currency. China currently manipulates the currency to keep it from getting too strong vs. the dollar, but in the future we expect China to flex its muscle and overcome the US Dollar in a bid to become the world's reserve currency, or at least a major player.

Lastly, you also might try the Guinness Atkinson Renminbi Yuan & Bond (GARBX) fund. On its website Guiness Atkinson states that the fund: "Seeks total return by investing in Renminbi Yuan bonds and cash deposits issued by the Chinese government and multinational corporations." The good part of this is that the Chinese bonds seem to be very appealing when thinking about a dollar reset where the resulting value is based on natural reserves, manufacturing, debt load and export capacity. The bad part is the 'multi-national corporations' that will not go through the dollar devaluation unscathed.

While we expect that multinational corporations will initially take a hit, we also suspect that GARBX will be heavily invested in Chinese based corporations that will only sag temporarily. An added attraction is the bonds are Chinese government bonds and pay interest upon maturity. GARBX is particularly attractive because you would get a favorable exchange rate after devaluation, added interest from the bonds, and it is investing in (what we believe is) the premier nation of the post-crash economy. All in all, this seems to be a good investment prospect.

Offshore Investing

Offshore investing is complicated and is scrutinized by the US Government extensively because of its reputed ties to supporting terrorism and illegal money 'laundering' (the practice of keeping one's accounting books and transactions from government eyes). The laws that have been put into place have made it difficult to move your money to a foreign country. In the words of Peter Schiff:

"I think we've already got the beginnings of capital controls in the United States. The government is making it very difficult for Americans to do business abroad. Many foreign financial institutions, banks, and even bullion depositories are refusing to do business with American citizens for fear of retaliation by the IRS or other government agencies."

So if you are considering moving your money to a bank that has less governmental transparency, then you might want to consider renouncing your citizenship. However, if you want to renounce your citizenship you have to fill out a form; forms used to be free. Now they're $500 apiece. To add insult to injury you can only get them from a foreign embassy or consulate. It is almost like the US government is trying to penalize its citizens for renouncing their citizenship. Again, this is the type of thing that the Nazis did to the Jews fleeing Nazi Germany.

If you are thinking on moving your money & precious assets offshore, then you might want to think about getting a team of lawyers first.

Getting Out of Dodge: Leaving the Country

At this point there are some who think about leaving the country. From a religious standpoint I personally hold the controversial position that the Bible is clear that we are told to leave a country that is under judgment; but that is just me and my opinion on this is beyond the scope of this paper. Given that, let's take a look at some of the things to consider if you are contemplating leaving the country.

First, if you are going to leave the country you need to do this now. The Foreign Account Tax Compliance Act (FATCA) is a United States statute that requires United

States persons, including individuals who live outside the United States, to report their financial accounts held outside of the United States, and requires foreign financial institutions to report to the Internal Revenue Service (IRS) about their American clients. Congress enacted FATCA to make it more difficult for U.S. taxpayers to conceal assets held in offshore accounts and shell corporations and to recoup federal tax revenues. Read another way, the IRS is saying that you can run and you cannot hide, we will get our pound of flesh from you wherever you are. This act goes into effect on July 1, 2014.

If you are thinking of running off to Canada, Costa Rica, Switzerland, or Mexico; think again. The IRS has treaties in place to tax you there. As of this writing there are some 48 countries that have agreements with the US/IRS, this administration is working very hard to sign agreements with more nations, and the ineffectual Republicans are 'trying' to repeal it (I sometimes wonder how genuine these efforts are because I see massive political vulnerabilities exposed by the Democrats that are ignored by the Republican party). Panama, Belize and Andorra are still options to go to without the IRS spying on your bank account, but check this before you do as this list is changing.

Most countries require that you have a job or a specific income level to expatriate, and some are pretty picky. No one wants to take on poor immigrants. But being 'rich' in a poor country might not be a good thing either. If a worldwide depression hits then poor people seeing 'rich' American Expats moving in will see targets for burglary, robbery, and kidnapping. This is particularly true for South American countries along the drug routes to the United States. You need to do some research before you select; just don't make your mind up based on an article you read on the internet.

Also note that the US government wants you to tell them if you are taking more than $10,000 out of the country. If you take more than $10,000 of your money out of the country and do not fill out FinCEN form 105 you will be a criminal according to The Department of the Treasury Financial Crimes Enforcement Network.

Silly you, you just thought that you could pick up and leave and take all of your earned belongings with you. Not so, because in the minds of the federal bureaucrats you are taking value away from the US; value where they think they have a right to part of it. Somehow in their demented logic it is OK to ship multi-million dollar factories and inventories overseas leaving the US worker out on the streets, but when the common man takes his nest egg to another country to retire the tax man is there to get 'what you owe him'.

The bottom line is that although the world will likely suffer in an upcoming economic collapse, the US will be at the bottom of the barrel – and the central bankers know this. That is why they are planning and making policies to benefit them in a post-crash economy. Moving to another country will be moving away from a lot of the social upheaval, but not all of it. Expect to have some economic discomfort wherever you go for some time until this world stabilizes.

Also, running the traps to get out of this country legally will likely cost you as this government is making it very difficult to exit with your belongings. Make no mistake about it, these people in banking/government know that chaos is on the horizon and they will need as much (scarce) money they can lay their hands on to keep their federal job afloat. They intend to take it from anyone who has money. Pensions will be 'nationalized', and personal finances will be taxed for the privilege of getting out of the country. This is the same mindset that took money from the Jews leaving Nazi Germany. People who have worked all their lives and paid taxes to build this country will be the hardest hit as the non-producing leeches seek the last drops of financial blood available to survive.

Timing the Devaluation

One of the most difficult things to do is to time such an event. Many people (yours truly included) might be right on track, but miss the boat on when things will happen and are usually early in forecasting financial events. We get the fundamentals right, but miss the timing because the big dogs of the financial world have all the short term controls that they exercise with neither apparent logic nor remorse.

In a larger context mere mortals like us see things like losing accounts of billions of dollars as a bad thing that brings on dire consequences, but in 2007 the Federal Reserve 'lost' some $500 billion and later in 2009 Ben Bernanke testified that he didn't know where the money went. He did this with a straight and uncaring face, and there were no consequences of his actions.

The inability of our congress to hold these criminals accountable is disgusting.

Misplacing a half trillion of US Taxpayer dollars without remorse is incomprehensible to the average man; but these people live in a world so far removed from reality that we cannot comprehend things as they do. So we cannot observe an event like committing to Quantitative Easing through common sense eyes that say printing hundreds of billions of dollars out of thin air will immediately cause something bad. What we can do is watch what these people are doing to protect themselves to see what is going on and what will happen next. But there is a problem here because the big dogs don't want people to know what they are doing.

There are rumors that the G20 made moves to devalue the dollar, and some of the rumor seems to be substantiated by the statement: "Exchange-rate flexibility can also facilitate the adjustment of our economies"; which supports a near term exchange rate split that would act a devaluation of the dollar. It also seems to be validated by Russian billionaires exiting all dollar denominated investments, and CEOs dumping stocks.

What all this means is that we believe that we are right in the fundamental nature of our economy – we are broke, printing money out of thin air to buy time, the not-so-indebted nations of the world are fed up with our shenanigans, and the (domestic) dollar must be split and devalued to stabilize international (dollar) trade. We stand and watch the big dogs try to hold back the tide, but market forces will ultimately prevail. Until then we can only observe and guess when the dam will break – but we think it is soon, based on what we see as the central banks positioning themselves for a post-US dollar world economy.

Summary

If you read news articles on the economy, debt, and financial movements within the global community the angst is so thick you can almost feel it. Something is going on and it's not good. Countries are buying up gold, demanding gold back from vaults and not getting it, the US is printing up billions upon billions of dollars that go into a black hole, and accountants sweat over of hundreds of trillions of dollars in unregulated derivatives that could explode at any moment. Economic officials of other countries are already talking about a post-dollar collapse economy and they are planning for it.

So should you.

All the major indicators that we follow are showing us that the dollar will be devalued, and that a temporary reserve dollar will be the recognized standard. With the dollar devaluation (reset) comes the destruction of the US economy, and a severe slowdown (and likely depression) of the world's economy.

If your nest egg gets caught in a dollar devaluation event it will likely be crushed, just like a little birds egg.

...Talk to your financial advisor, review your investments, and stay as safe as you can.

For The Madison Institute Association

To understand more on how debt and corruption works get **Anger to Action**: Understanding American Debt, Corruption, and Inflation... And What is Needed to Save the Republic; it is also available in <u>Kindle</u> format.

Dennis Stapp is an author, inventor, and graduated with honors in Physics from the University of Southern Mississippi. He has studied law, private investigation, and was a founding member of The Madison Institute Association (an organization that has been promoting American liberties since the 80's and formally incorporated as an association in 2010). He has lectured on government corruption, natural disasters, applied Christianity, and our fraudulent economy for the better part of three decades. He is a system analyst that lives in Madison Alabama with his wife and two children.